Writing Resource Guide

Rigby®
A Harcourt Achieve Imprint

www.Rigby.com
1-800-531-5015

Contents

Using the Grammar Lessons and the Writer's Handbook

Grammar is an essential element in effective writing. Without this fundamental knowledge, children cannot convey their message to an audience.

Lesson Background
- Provides an explanation of the grammar skill.

Teaching the Lesson
- Direct, explicit instruction on the conventions that need to be mastered.

- Refers to the Writer's Handbook for definitions, examples, and grammar rules.

Extending the Lesson
- Reinforces and applies the strategies and techniques targeted during Teaching the Lesson.

On Your Own
- Provides children with an opportunity to practice the skill on their own or with partners.

Theme 2

Complete Sentence: Begins with a Capital Letter

You Will Need
- Writer's Handbook, page 4
- chart paper and marker
- paper and pencil for each child
- storybooks for examples

Lesson Background
The first letter of the first word in a sentence is always capitalized. Capital letters alert a reader to the start of a new sentence.

Teaching the Lesson
- To introduce starting sentences with capitals, read aloud the relevant portion of page 4 of the Writer's Handbook as children follow along.
- Write a capital *D* and a lowercase *d* on chart paper. Ask a child to explain how they differ. Review the terms *capital* and *lowercase* if necessary.
- Write the following sentences on chart paper: *The tree is big. My ball is red. I like school.* Read the sentences aloud.
- Have volunteers circle the capital letters. Ask children what pattern they see in the capital letters in the sentences.
- Ask a child to make up another sentence to add to the chart paper. Write the sentence he or she creates, drawing attention to the capital letter in the first word.
- Explain the use of capitals at the beginning of sentences. *All sentences begin with capital letters.*

Extending the Lesson
Write the sentences in the margin on chart paper. Ask children to find the lowercase letters at the beginning of the sentences. Have children rewrite the sentences on paper, beginning each with a capital letter.

On Your Own
Have children look at one page of a storybook to find the capital letters at the beginning of sentences. Encourage early finishers to look at other pages.

we play at school.
lisa helps me.
it is fun!

Assess Progress
Note children's ability to identify capital letters and correctly place them at the beginning of sentences. Provide additional practice if necessary.

4 Theme 2   Complete Sentence: Begins with a Capital Letter

Using the Writer's Handbook
The Writer's Handbook is a valuable reference book for both teachers and children. It can be used with the grammar focus lessons in this guide or to introduce grade-level grammar skills. As children become familiar with grammar, they can use this book as a reference to answer questions about spelling, capitalization, grammar, and usage.

The Writer's Handbook is:

- For teachers to use as they teach focus lessons on grammar, usage, and mechanics during writing instruction.

- For children to use during the Writing Workshop.

Using the Writing Organizers

The Writing Organizers are reproducible graphic organizers that children use, first in groups and then individually, to develop concepts during prewriting. They are a basic framework for children's compositions. Before children use the Writing Organizers, they have participated in the shared writing process with a teacher using the Writing Charts. The Writing Organizer duplicates the graphic organizer used on the Writing Chart.

Each Writing Workshop focuses on an organizational pattern or a writing form. When featured in explicit instruction, writing forms act as an important supportive frame in which students compose their own ideas. The Writing Organizers provide a hands-on, visual framework to help students organize their ideas and plan their writing.

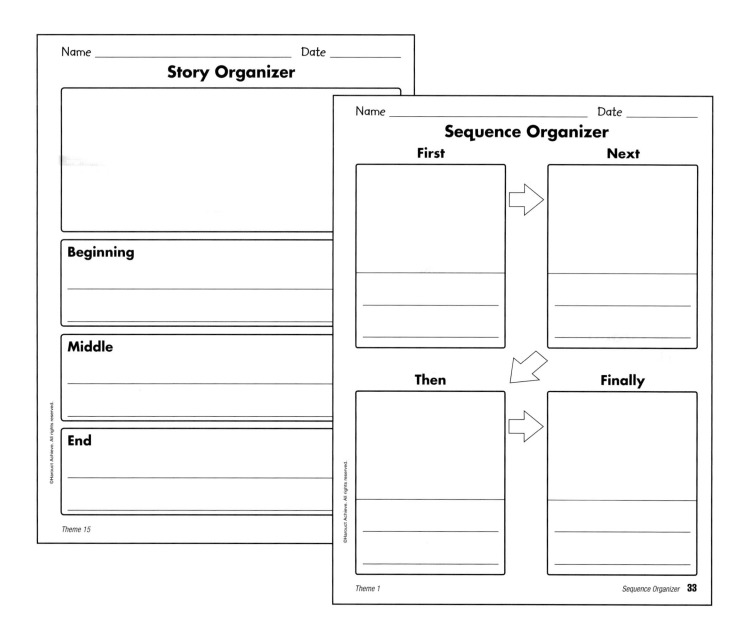

Using the Writer's Craft Lessons

Attention to writer's craft – which covers a host of tools and topics – is an essential way to improve children's writing while reinforcing the notion that the writing process is a craft.

Lesson Background
- Defines the Writer's Craft strategy.

Teaching the Lesson
- Focuses on selections (on the blackline master) that provide a model of the strategy to be addressed in the lesson.

- Guided instruction allows children to analyze and practice the targeted skill in a whole group setting.

Extending the Lesson
- Reinforces skills, strategies, and techniques in small groups or independent writing.

- Focuses on applying the craft skill to children's own work.

On Your Own
- Provides practice in the skill individually or with a partner.

- Encourages the use of the Writer's Notebook.

Whole Group Activity
- Provides a text and an activity for children to practice the craft skill.

- The blackline master can be copied or made into a transparency for instruction.

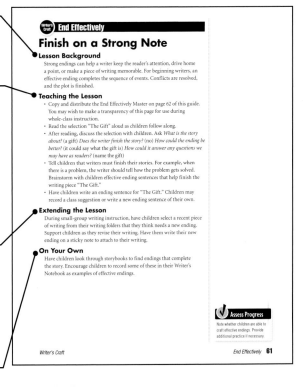

Writer's Craft — **End Effectively**

Finish on a Strong Note

Lesson Background
Strong endings can help a writer keep the reader's attention, drive home a point, or make a piece of writing memorable. For beginning writers, an effective ending completes the sequence of events. Conflicts are resolved, and the plot is finished.

Teaching the Lesson
- Copy and distribute the End Effectively Master on page 62 of this guide. You may wish to make a transparency of this page for use during whole-class instruction.
- Read the selection "The Gift" aloud as children follow along.
- After reading, discuss the selection with children. Ask *What is the story about?* (a gift) *Does the writer finish the story?* (no) *How could the ending be better?* (it could say what the gift is) *How could it answer any questions we may have as readers?* (name the gift)
- Tell children that writers must finish their stories. For example, when there is a problem, the writer should tell how the problem gets solved. Brainstorm with children effective ending sentences that help finish the writing piece "The Gift."
- Have children write an ending sentence for "The Gift." Children may record a class suggestion or write a new ending sentence of their own.

Extending the Lesson
During small-group writing instruction, have children select a recent piece of writing from their writing folders that they think needs a new ending. Support children as they revise their writing. Have them write their new ending on a sticky note to attach to their writing.

On Your Own
Have children look through storybooks to find endings that complete the story. Encourage children to record some of these in their Writer's Notebook as examples of effective endings.

✓ **Assess Progress**
Note whether children are able to craft effective endings. Provide additional practice if necessary.

Writer's Craft — End Effectively **61**

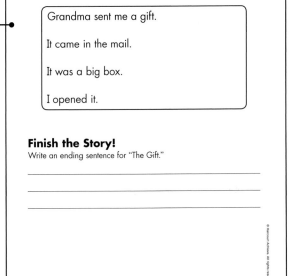

The Gift

Grandma sent me a gift.

It came in the mail.

It was a big box.

I opened it.

Finish the Story!
Write an ending sentence for "The Gift."

_____

_____

_____

62 *Writer's Craft* — End Effectively Master

Writing Assessment Rubric

The *Literacy by Design* Writing Assessment Rubric contains key behavioral indicators for holistically evaluating the development of young writers. Use the rubric not only to identify the developmental stage of your students but also to plot their future growth, both within and across stages. (See the Writing Assessment Rubric Form on page xi.)

	Experimenting Stage	Emerging Stage
Content Ideas and Organization	• Scribbles emulate the look of writing; some may carry meaning. • Simple illustrations represent ideas. • Student shares ideas orally; ideas may lack focus and may vary upon subsequent retellings. • Student may attempt organization by grouping scribbles or illustrations together.	• Illustrations begin to have more detail. • Student orally explains ideas and may elaborate on illustrations or written words and phrases. • Some ideas begin to take shape, but a clear message or storyline may not be present. • Organization continues to develop as student groups similar words and illustrations. • With prompting, student can state audience and purpose.
Language Sentence Fluency, Word Choice, and Voice	• Student shows an awareness that illustrations and written words are different. • Student knows letters and begins to experiment with sound-letter relationships, although some letters may be random. • Illustrations represent common words and generally lack distinguishing features.	• Student demonstrates understanding of one-to-one correspondence between written and spoken words (e.g., student points while reading). • Writing takes the form of simple, common words, phrases, or sentences. • Voice begins to emerge as student adds personal touches to writing and illustrations.
Mechanics Writing Conventions	• Student begins to show an awareness of left-right writing directionality. • Student writes strings of letters and may begin to group letters into words, whether pretend or actual. • Writing is not always legible.	• Clear words emerge, with proper spacing. • Student experiments with uppercase and lowercase letters. • Student begins to group words together into phrases and sentences, arranging them from left to right. • A number of words may be spelled phonetically.
Process Writing Purpose, Process, and Presentation	• Student relies on teacher prompting to draw or "write" about a specific idea. • Student talks about (or explains) work and can be prompted to add to it (e.g., can add more details to a drawing). • Final work may be scattered and disordered on page; illustrations may be labeled.	• Student understands the purpose of and relies upon a small number of text forms (e.g., story, letter). • With guidance, student talks to generate ideas for writing. • Student draws pictures or writes words/phrases about a specific idea. • Student can be prompted to add to the work and make simple corrections. • Final work is mostly legible and more organized; clear use of simple fiction and nonfiction text features (e.g., labels, titles) emerges.

Developing Stage	Proficient Stage	Advanced Stage
• Illustrations, if present, begin to support writing rather than substitute for writing. • A message or storyline is present but may lack a clear beginning or a clear ending. • Some ideas are supported with details but may lack focus. • Ideas show a more formal attempt at organization; some sequencing and use of simple transitions (e.g., words such as *next* or *then*) may be present.	• A clear message or storyline is present, with a serviceable beginning and ending. • Ideas are focused and supported with sufficient details; some details may be weak or off topic. • Ideas are generally well organized; student begins to use more complex transitions to achieve greater passage-level coherence (e.g., transitions that link key content and ideas from sentence to sentence). • Student begins to make choices about ideas and organization to suit audience and purpose.	• A clear message or storyline is present, with an engaging beginning and ending. • Ideas are focused and fully supported with strong, relevant details. • Ideas are well organized; use of transitions and other devices results in writing that is smooth, coherent, and easy to follow. • Student makes strong, effective choices about ideas and organization to suit audience and purpose.
• Simple and compound sentences are used in writing. • Student begins to experiment with different sentence types and syntactical patterns that aid fluency, but overall writing may still be choppy. • Student correctly uses and relies upon a small bank of mostly common words; student may begin to experiment with less common words. • More frequent hints of voice and personality are present, but writing continues to be mostly mechanical.	• More fluent writing emerges through the use of an increasing variety of sentence types and syntactical patterns. • Student correctly uses a large bank of common words; student effectively experiments with new words and begins to choose words more purposefully (e.g., to create images or to have an emotional impact). • Voice continues to develop as student experiments with language.	• All sentence types are present. • Student writes fluently, varying sentence types, sentence beginnings, and grammatical structures. • Student uses an extensive bank of common and less common words correctly; student successfully uses words with precision and purpose. • Voice is expressive, engaging, and appropriate to audience and purpose.
• Sentences have beginning capitalization and ending punctuation; student experiments with other marks (e.g., commas). • Paragraphing begins to emerge. • Spelling is more conventional, especially for high frequency words. • Awareness of usage (i.e., that there are rules to be followed) begins to develop; student experiments with simple usage conventions, but success is variable.	• Student correctly uses all marks of end punctuation; correct use of some other marks is evident, especially in typical situations (e.g., a comma before the conjunction in a compound sentence or a colon to introduce a list). • Student correctly spells most high frequency words and begins to transfer spelling "rules" to lesser-known words. • Writing demonstrates basic understanding of standard grade-level grammar and usage.	• Student correctly and effectively uses standard grade-level punctuation, including more sophisticated marks and usages (e.g., dashes to emphasize key ideas). • Student correctly spells a wide variety of words, both common and uncommon. • Writing demonstrates full and effective control of standard grade-level grammar and usage; overall usage aids reading.
• Student experiments with a variety of text forms and begins to understand how purpose determines form. • Student generates limited prewriting ideas. • With teacher support, draft shows some development but continues to be mostly skeletal. • Student revisits the work but mostly to correct a few line-level errors (e.g., end punctuation and spelling). • Student begins to move more naturally and independently through the writing process. • Final work is generally neat; an increasing variety of fiction and nonfiction text features (e.g., titles, headings, charts, captions) is present, but features may be more for show than for support of message.	• Student demonstrates increasing control over a variety of text forms and can choose form to suit purpose. • Student generates sufficient prewriting ideas. • Draft shows good development of prewriting, including effective attempts at focusing, organizing, and elaborating ideas. • Student revisits the work not only to correct errors but also to address some passage-level issues (e.g., clarity of message, sufficiency of details); student may use supporting resources (e.g., dictionary, grammar book). • Sense that the process is purposeful begins to emerge. • Final work is neat; use of various fiction and nonfiction text features tends to support and clarify meaning.	• Student effectively controls a variety of text forms and can choose form to suit purpose. • Student uses prewriting ideas as a plan that is both general and flexible. • Draft shows strong development of prewriting and may effectively depart from prewriting as a signal of the student's overall writing maturity. • Student revisits the work not only to correct errors but also to address key passage-level issues. • Overall, student shows investment in the craft of writing and moves through the stages smoothly and recursively. • Final work is neat; effective use of fiction and nonfiction text features results in a polish that strengthens the student's overall message.

Snapshots of Young Writers

Writing samples, or anchor papers, provide powerful snapshots of writing development—snapshots key to understanding students' control over written language and to determining subsequent paths of instruction. The following writing samples represent each of the five stages of development in the *Literacy by Design* Writing Assessment Rubric. The samples for each stage are preceded by a brief summary of key behavioral indicators for that stage.

Experimenting Stage

- Writing is mostly an attempt to emulate adult writing.
- It includes single letters, letter strings, and simple illustrations.
- Writing attempts to be communicative, but most letters and letter strings do not carry consistent meaning.

Nour

Mireya

Emerging Stage

- Writing shows an understanding that spoken words can be written down and read by others.
- It includes the use of content-bearing words, phrases, and short sentences.
- Writing may demonstrate left-right directionality and experimentation with capital letters and end marks.
- It includes many words spelled phonetically.

Ricky

Caden

Developing Stage

- Writing exhibits growing control over writing conventions, including more conventional spelling, punctuation, and grammar.
- Writing carries a simple message supported by some details.
- Sentence structure is mostly formulaic and mechanical.
- It includes a limited number of text forms.

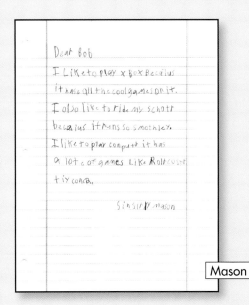

Mason

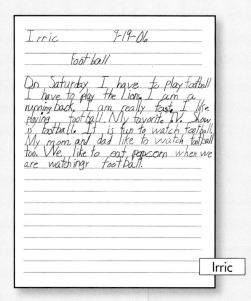

Irric

Proficient Stage

- Writing includes a clear, focused message supported by sufficient details.
- It exhibits most grade-level conventions.
- Writing includes a variety of sentence structures.
- It shows a growing awareness of audience and purpose.
- It demonstrates control over a variety of text forms.

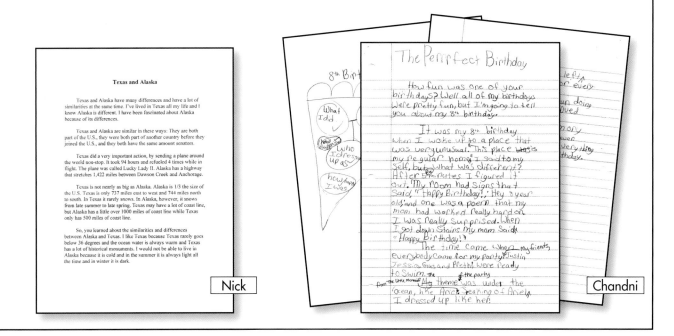

Nick

Chandni

Advanced Stage

- Writing demonstrates mastery of conventions and purposeful variety of sentence structures.
- It includes a strong, focused message that is fully supported and engaging in presentation.
- Writing exhibits a clear understanding of audience and purpose.
- It shows effective use of word choice, voice, details, and text form.

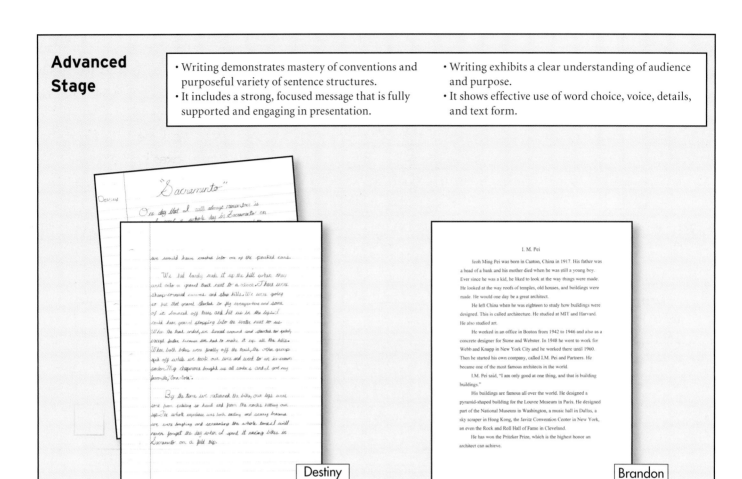

Destiny

Brandon

Writing Stages According to Grade Level

	Experimenting Stage	Emerging Stage	Developing Stage	Proficient Stage	Advanced Stage
Grade K	▓▓▓▓▓				
Grade 1		▓▓▓▓▓			
Grade 2			▓▓▓▓		
Grade 3				▓▓▓	
Grade 4				▓▓▓▓	
Grade 5				▓▓▓▓▓▓	

Writing Assessment Rubric Form

Student's Name _____   **Date** _____

(1)
- Based on an initial review of a representative sampling of student work, identify the student's most likely stage of development. Locate that stage on the rubric and then review the behavioral indicators for each of the four instructional categories: Content, Language, Mechanics, and Process.
- If the indicators for a particular category mostly describe the student's work, check the appropriate box.
- The student is considered to be in a particular stage if at least three category boxes in that stage have been checked. If fewer than three boxes are checked, the student is considered to be in the previous stage.

	Experimenting	Emerging	Developing	Proficient	Advanced
Content Ideas and Organization	☐	☐	☐	☐	☐
Language Sentence Fluency, Word Choice, and Voice	☐	☐	☐	☐	☐
Mechanics Writing Conventions	☐	☐	☐	☐	☐
Process Writing Purpose, Process, and Presentation	☐	☐	☐	☐	☐

Stage _____

(2)
- Note observations about key strengths and weaknesses.
- Tie observations to specific strategies to be used in future instruction.

Observations	Notes for Future Instruction
Strengths	
Growth Areas	

* It is recommended that you use the *Literacy by Design* Writing Assessment Rubric to evaluate a sampling of each student's writing at least three times a year.

Managing Writing Workshop

Independent Writing at the Core

Similar to reading workshop, writing workshop is the time when a teacher works with a small group of students to differentiate writing instruction. Other students are engaged in writing independently, whether that means generating ideas, writing a draft, or revising their writing.

Students learn to write with practice. They need ample classroom time to explore ideas and refine their writing skills. Independent writing allows students to apply the strategies and skills they are learning in whole class and small group instruction.

A key difference between small group writing and small group reading is that student writers are typically working on the same piece as they move from the group to independent work. In fact, a writer might continue work on the same writing piece over several small group sessions, continuing to work on the piece between sessions in independent writing as well. Having the two activities occur simultaneously in the same workshop emphasizes the connection between small group and independent writing.

Making Independent Writing Successful

- **Conference regularly with writers**. Meet with students to ensure they use their Writer's Notebook or other resources when recording ideas and finding writing topics (See *Comprehensive Teacher's Guide*, Writing Conference Form, page A23).

- **Provide a focus for independent writing**. Choose a writing form, organizational pattern, process, or trait that is taught in the theme to serve as a focus for students during independent writing.

- **Offer prompts when writers get stuck**. The best source for writing ideas is a student's Writer's Notebook, but occasionally students just get stuck. Provide specific prompts related to the theme's instructional focus that can be used when students are having difficulty identifying a topic for their writing.

Setting Up Writing Workshop

In a successful writing workshop, students understand and embrace the opportunity to explore ideas and mold those ideas into text. Planning requires setting up materials and creating an environment in which students can manage their independent writing time effectively.

Create a Space for a Successful Writing Workshop

- Designated place for students to keep their **writing folders** and **Writer's Notebooks**

- **Reference area** with dictionaries, encyclopedias, and thesauruses

- **Writing center** with magazines and other visual materials to spark ideas

- Wall space to display **shared** and **interactive writing pieces**

- Copies of **graphic organizers** to capture and organize writing ideas (see pages 33–48)

Words Make Sentences; Word Spacing

Lesson Background

Sentences are groups of words that together express a complete thought. Emphasize that words in a sentence should be separated by an appropriate amount of space. Proper word spacing is vital for clarity in written English.

Teaching the Lesson

- To introduce sentences, read aloud the relevant portion of page 4 of the Writer's Handbook as children follow along.
- Ask for two volunteers. Give each child an index card with one of these words: *Dan* and *runs*. Say to each child *You are a word*. Place each child in order so the class can see the sentence *Dan runs*. Ask a volunteer to read it aloud. Explain that words in a group make a sentence. Then sweep your hand in front of the two children and say *You are a sentence*.
- Write the sentence on chart paper, leaving out the space: *Danruns*. Ask *What is wrong with this sentence?* Rewrite, leaving one finger space between the words. Ask *Which sentence is easier to read?*
- Then repeat with the same sentence, leaving too much space between the words.
- Define sentences and explain sentence and word spacing. *Sentences are groups of words that tell us an idea. We need to leave space between the words so people can read the sentence. But if we leave too much space, the words will be hard to read.*

Extending the Lesson

Write the sentences in the margin on chart paper. Give children the following directions: *Give a thumbs-up if the sentence words have the right amount of space. Give a thumbs-down if the sentence words do not have the right amount of space.* Read aloud the sentences one at a time.

On Your Own

Have children look through a storybook. Ask them to select a sentence and copy it onto a piece of paper of their own. Remind them to leave one finger space between the words.

You Will Need

- Writer's Handbook, page 4
- chart paper and marker
- index cards with the following words written on them: *Dan* and *runs*
- paper and pencil for each child
- storybooks for sentence examples

Bob runs.

Dadeats.

The frog hops.

Assess Progress

Note children's ability to form complete sentences and space words properly. Provide additional practice if necessary.

Word Order (Subject, Verb, Object)

Lesson Background

Rules govern the order of sentence parts (*i.e.*, subject, verb, and object). In declarative sentences, subjects come first, verbs follow subjects, and objects, if any are present, come last.

Teaching the Lesson

- To introduce sentence word order, read aloud the relevant portion of page 5 of the Writer's Handbook as children follow along.
- Ask for three volunteers. Give each child an index card with one of these words: *Tran, walks, home.* Have children hold up their cards and stand in sentence order. Read the sentence aloud: *Tran walks home.*
- Ask *Who walks home?* (Tran) Ask a second question: *What does Tran do?* (walks home) Ask a third question: *Where did Tran go?* (home)
- Rearrange children holding the index cards so that together they read *home walks Tran.* Ask children if the sentence still works. Explain that home cannot walk Tran, so the words do not make a sentence anymore.
- Repeat with the index cards for *Liz plays ball.*
- Explain sentence order. *Sentences have parts. The parts need to be in the right order or the sentence won't make sense.*

Extending the Lesson

Write the sentences in the margin on chart paper and read them aloud. Ask children to put the sentences in order. Write the correct sentences on the chart paper. *(Mom comes home. Sam is big. Dad has a car.)*

On Your Own

Ask children to write a three-word sentence on a sheet of paper. Check children's sentences and redirect as necessary. Instruct children to cut apart the words of their sentences. Have them work in pairs to put each other's words in the correct order.

home comes Mom.

big is Sam.

a car has Dad.

Assess Progress

Note children's ability to put words in proper order. Provide additional practice if necessary.

Complete Sentence Has a Complete Thought

Lesson Background

Complete sentences are formed when a subject and a predicate are grouped. If either component is missing, the words form a fragment.

Teaching the Lesson

- To introduce complete sentences, read aloud the relevant portion of page 4 of the Writer's Handbook as children follow along.
- Write these words on chart paper: *The cat*. Read aloud the words. Ask *Is this a sentence?* Have children explain their decision. Then write: *The cat sat on the hat*. Read the sentence aloud. Ask *Is this a sentence?* Have children explain their decision.
- Identify *The cat* as the naming part of the sentence. Identify *sat on the hat* as the telling part. Explain that sentences are not complete unless they have a naming part and a telling part.
- Ask a volunteer to explain why *The cat* is not a complete sentence. Encourage use of the terms *naming part* and *telling part* in his or her answer.
- Explain complete sentences. *Sentences must have naming parts and telling parts to be complete. Naming parts tell who or what the sentence is about. Telling parts tell what that person or thing does.*

Extending the Lesson

Tape word strips on the board that show either the naming or telling parts of sentences. Ask volunteers to read the words on the strips. Have children come up, move, and join the strips to create complete sentences.

On Your Own

Write the phrases in the margin on chart paper. Have children copy them and decide if each is a sentence. Ask children to finish any sentences that are incomplete.

You Will Need

- Writer's Handbook, page 4
- chart paper and marker
- word strips reading: *The ball/ is red./ My dad/ likes cats./ We/ play tag.*
- tape
- paper and pencil for each child

The dog

plays games.

The pen

Assess Progress

Note whether children can recognize and produce complete sentences. Provide additional practice if necessary.

Complete Sentence: Begins with a Capital Letter

Lesson Background

The first letter of the first word in a sentence is always capitalized. Capital letters alert a reader to the start of a new sentence.

Teaching the Lesson

- To introduce starting sentences with capitals, read aloud the relevant portion of page 4 of the Writer's Handbook as children follow along.
- Write a capital *D* and a lowercase *d* on chart paper. Ask a child to explain how they differ. Review the terms *capital* and *lowercase* if necessary.
- Write the following sentences on chart paper: *The tree is big. My ball is red. I like school.* Read the sentences aloud.
- Have volunteers circle the capital letters. Ask children what pattern they see in the capital letters in the sentences.
- Ask a child to make up another sentence to add to the chart paper. Write the sentence he or she creates, drawing attention to the capital letter in the first word.
- Explain the use of capitals at the beginning of sentences. *All sentences begin with capital letters.*

we play at school.

lisa helps me.

it is fun!

Extending the Lesson

Write the sentences in the margin on chart paper. Ask children to find the lowercase letters at the beginning of the sentences. Have children rewrite the sentences on paper, beginning each with a capital letter.

On Your Own

Have children look at one page of a storybook to find the capital letters at the beginning of sentences. Encourage early finishers to look at other pages.

Assess Progress

Note children's ability to identify capital letters and correctly place them at the beginning of sentences. Provide additional practice if necessary.

Ending Punctuation

Lesson Background

Complete sentences end with a period, an exclamation point, or a question mark. Ending punctuation alerts a reader that an idea is complete.

Teaching the Lesson

- To introduce ending punctuation, read aloud the relevant portions of pages 4 and 8 of the Writer's Handbook as children follow along.
- Tell children that every sentence needs to end with a punctuation mark. Ask a volunteer to name the punctuation mark that comes at the end of a question. Have the child draw a question mark on the chart paper. Ask a volunteer to name the punctuation mark that we use at the end of sentences that show we're really excited. Have the child draw an exclamation point on the chart paper. Ask a volunteer to name the punctuation mark that we put at the end of most sentences. Have the child draw a period on the chart paper.
- Write *I saw a cat* on chart paper. Read it aloud so children can hear that it is a statement. Say *My sentence tells something. I'll use a period.* Add a period.
- Continue the instruction with *Do you like cats* and *Cats are fun.* Read with exaggerated expression to help children recognize each type of sentence. Have children suggest the appropriate punctuation marks.
- Explain the need to use punctuation to end sentences. *Sentences end with punctuation marks. Ending punctuation marks include periods, question marks, and exclamation points.*

Extending the Lesson

Write the paragraph in the margin on chart paper, leaving space after each sentence for the insertion of a punctuation mark. Then read it aloud. After each sentence, have children suggest which punctuation mark to insert.

On Your Own

Ask children to write a sentence without punctuation. Remind them that they can write a question or an exclamation. Divide the class into pairs. Have each child read aloud his or her sentence to his or her partner. Remind children to use expression to help their partners understand if their sentences are questions or exclamations. Partners should then punctuate each other's sentences.

You Will Need

- Writer's Handbook, pages 4 and 8
- chart paper and marker
- paper and pencil for each child

Pets are good ____

I love dogs and cats ____

I dont like snakes ____

Do you have pets ____

 Assess Progress

Note whether children recognize the need to end sentences with punctuation. Provide additional practice if necessary.

Review Simple Sentences

Lesson Background

A simple sentence is a group of words that expresses a complete idea. It includes a subject, a verb, and possibly an object. It begins with a capital letter and ends with a period, a question mark, or an exclamation point. Sentences must have the appropriate amount of space between each word.

Teaching the Lesson

- To review simple sentences, read aloud the relevant portions of pages 4, 5, and 8 of the Writer's Handbook as children follow along.
- Write the following sentence on chart paper: *Jess plays tag.* Ask children to explain why this is a sentence. Guide the discussion to cover the following: it has a naming part and a telling part, it starts with a capital letter, and it ends with a period.
- Ask children to identify the naming part. Underline *Jess* in one color. Ask them to identify the telling part. Underline *plays tag* in a second color.
- Repeat with the sentences *Ron runs* and *We love dogs!*
- Ask children what the *j* in Jess, the *r* in Ron, and the *w* in *We* have in common. Circle the capital letters in a third color and remind children that sentences begin with a capital letter.
- Ask children what the ends of the three sentences have in common. Circle the punctuation marks. Remind children that sentences end with punctuation.
- Explain to children the basic elements of simple sentences. *A sentence tells a complete idea. It starts with a capital letter and includes a naming part and a telling part. Sentences end with a punctuation mark: a period, a question mark, or an exclamation point.*

Extending the Lesson

Tape the following word strips on the board: *he, Ted, the baby, runs, hops, has a ball.* Ask a volunteer to read aloud a sentence combining two strips. Ask him or her to come up to the board and write the full sentence, using a capital letter and a punctuation mark.

On Your Own

Ask children to make two more sentences by combining the rest of the word strips. Tell them to write the sentences down, using a capital letter and a punctuation mark.

You Will Need

- Writer's Handbook, pages 4, 5, and 8
- word strips with the following written on them: *he, Ted, the baby, runs, hops, has a ball*
- chart paper and three different-colored markers
- paper and pencil for each child
- tape

Jess plays tag.

Ron runs.

We love dogs!

 **Assess Progress**

Note whether children can recognize and form simple sentences. Provide additional practice if necessary.

Telling Sentence

Lesson Background

A telling sentence makes a statement and ends with a period. The subject appears first, and the predicate comes after the subject. The predicate contains the verb and tells what someone or something is or does.

Teaching the Lesson

- To introduce telling sentences, read aloud the relevant portion of page 5 of the Writer's Handbook as children follow along.
- Write the parts of telling sentences as an idea web on chart paper. In the top bubble, write *Telling Sentences*. The three connecting bubbles should read *1) naming part; 2) telling part;* and *3) period*. Explain that telling sentences need these three parts in this order.
- Write on chart paper and read aloud the sentence: *I am big*. Underline *I* once and tell children this is the naming part. Underline *am big* twice and tell children this is the telling part. Circle the period. Ask children if the sentence has everything a telling sentence needs.
- Repeat the activity, having volunteers mark the sentence parts, with the following two sentences: *Mom likes cars. Tim plays tag.*
- Explain to children how to identify a telling sentence. *A telling sentence begins with a naming part. Then it has a telling part that tells what happens. Telling sentences end with a period.*

Extending the Lesson

Write the following on chart paper: *Where is Dad? Sits down. Mari and I.* Guide children to explain why these examples are not telling sentences. (ends with a question mark, has no naming part, has no telling part)

On Your Own

Ask children to find a telling sentence in a book and copy it onto a piece of paper. Have them underline the naming part once and the telling part twice and circle the period. Encourage early finishers to try to write their own telling sentences.

You Will Need

- Writer's Handbook, page 5
- chart paper and marker
- a book for each child written at his or her current reading level
- paper and pencil for each child

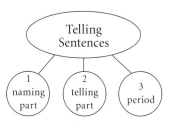

I am big.

Mom likes cars.

Tim plays tag.

Assess Progress

Note whether children can recognize telling sentences. Provide additional practice if necessary.

Asking Sentence

Lesson Background

An asking sentence asks a question and ends with a question mark. Asking sentences often begin with a question word: *who, what, where, when, why,* or *how.*

Teaching the Lesson

- To introduce asking sentences, read aloud the relevant portions of pages 5 and 8 of the Writer's Handbook as children follow along.
- Tell children that an asking sentence asks a question, ends in a question mark, and usually begins with a question word. Write a question mark on chart paper and name it. Write and read aloud this list of question words: *who, what, when, where, why, how.*
- Write these sentences on chart paper: *Who are you? Where is he? I like him.* Ask a volunteer to find the sentence that is not a question and explain his or her reasoning. Cross out the third sentence.
- Ask volunteers to think of asking sentences that begin with the question words listed on chart paper. Write three shared sentences on chart paper.
- Explain to children how to identify an asking sentence. *An asking sentence asks a question and ends with a question mark. Many asking sentences begin with the question words* who, what, when, where, why, *or* how.

Extending the Lesson

Tape the sentence fragment strips you have prepared on the board and place the index cards below them. Guide children to decide which question word makes sense for each sentence and tape it in place.

On Your Own

Ask children to write an asking sentence that begins with a question word and ends with a question mark. Challenge early finishers to write telling sentences to answer their questions.

You Will Need

- Writer's Handbook, pages 5 and 8
- chart paper and marker
- index cards with the words *who, what,* and *where* written on them
- sentence fragment strips with the following written on them: *is your pen? is your name? is your teacher?*
- tape
- paper and pencil for each child

Assess Progress

Note whether children can recognize and punctuate asking sentences. Provide additional practice if necessary.

Command/Express with End Punctuation

Lesson Background

Sentences that contain strong commands or intense emotion, such as surprise, anger, fear, or joy, are often punctuated with an exclamation point. The addition of an exclamation point signals increased force or intensity.

Teaching the Lesson

- To introduce commands and exclamation points, read aloud the relevant portions of pages 5 and 8 of the Writer's Handbook as children follow along.

- Write and label a period and an exclamation point on chart paper. Make a two-column chart with the headings *Commands* and *Strong Feelings*. Explain that a command is a sentence that tells someone to do something. Help children brainstorm items to go under the headings. (*Commands:* sit down, stop, pay attention, go; *Strong Feelings:* anger, surprise, fear, joy) Explain that sentences ending in exclamation points should be read with a louder voice.

- Write the following sentences on chart paper, omitting the punctuation: *I am six ___ I love recess ___ Get down ___ Tie your shoe ___*. Ask volunteers to complete the sentences with periods or exclamation points. Have them explain their choices. Then read the sentences with children using the appropriate tone to match the punctuation they have chosen.

- Explain the appropriate use of exclamation points. *A sentence should have an exclamation point if it shows a strong feeling or tells you to do something in a strong way.*

Extending the Lesson

Have children look through storybooks to find an example of a sentence that ends in an exclamation point. Have each child write down his or her sentence and decide whether it shows strong feelings or tells someone to do something in a strong way.

On Your Own

Ask children to write a sentence that ends with an exclamation point. Then have them read their sentences to a partner using the correct inflection.

You Will Need

- Writer's Handbook, pages 5 and 8
- chart paper and marker
- storybooks
- paper and pencil for each child

 Assess Progress

Check that children can recognize commands and sentences that require exclamation points. Provide additional practice if necessary.

Review Sentence Types

Lesson Background

Young writers must practice and master appropriate use of the four basic sentence types: telling, asking, commands, and exclamations. They should be able to use the appropriate end punctuation for each type of sentence.

Teaching the Lesson

- To review sentence types, read the relevant portions of pages 5 and 8 of the Writer's Handbook aloud as children follow along.
- Write the following on chart paper: *Max is five __ Quiet down __ How old are you __*. Ask children to tell which punctuation mark should be added to each sentence. Have children explain their choices.
- Write *It's Friday* on chart paper. Add a period to the end of the sentence and read it aloud. Say *Listen to how the meaning changes if the punctuation mark is changed*. Cross out the period, add an exclamation point, and reread. Explain how the meaning has changed. Repeat with a question mark, changing the sentence to *Is it Friday*? Point out the new word order.
- Ask children to explain telling sentences, asking sentences, commands, and sentences that have an exclamation point.
- Summarize the sentence types. *A telling sentence tells something and ends in a period. An asking sentence asks a question and ends with a question mark. A command tells someone to do something. Sentences that show strong feelings or tell someone to do something in a strong way end in exclamation points.*

Extending the Lesson

Divide children into groups of five to find examples of each of the four types of sentences in a book. Each group should choose one sentence to copy onto a sentence strip with crayons. Divide the board into four sections, with headings *Telling, Asking, Command*, and *Exclamation*. Have each group tape its chosen sentence in the correct area and read it aloud to the class.

On Your Own

Ask children to write a telling sentence, an asking sentence, a command, and a sentence that needs an exclamation point about their favorite book. Have three volunteers read their sentences aloud.

You Will Need

- Writer's Handbook, pages 5 and 8
- chart paper and marker
- blank sentence strips
- crayons or markers for each group
- tape
- paper and pencil for each child
- storybooks for sentence examples

 **Assess Progress**

Assess children's ability to recognize different sentence types. Provide additional practice if necessary.

Naming Words: Animals and Things (Common Nouns)

Lesson Background

A noun names a person, place, or thing. Common nouns are nonspecific and begin with lowercase letters. This lesson covers a subcategory of common nouns: animals and things.

Teaching the Lesson

- To introduce common nouns, read aloud the relevant portion of page 14 of the Writer's Handbook as children follow along.
- Write on chart paper and read aloud: *Naming words name a person, place, or thing.* Tell children that today they will learn about naming words for animals and things.
- Explain that naming words can be found anywhere in sentences. Write the following on chart paper and read the sentence aloud: *The frog sat on the log.* Ask children which word names an animal. Circle *frog*. Ask children if there are any more naming words in the sentence. Reread and check for nouns that name things. Circle *log*.
- Repeat the procedure for *The cat ran up the tree.*
- Pass out index cards you have prepared. Divide the board into two columns and write the headings *Animals* and *Things*. Have children come up one at a time and tape their cards in the correct column. Check the card placement together.
- Explain nouns to children. *A naming word is a word that names a person, animal, place, or thing.*

Extending the Lesson

Ask volunteers to make sentences using the nouns on the chart paper. Challenge children to create sentences that include naming words that name both animals and things.

On Your Own

Have children find one naming word that names an animal and one that names a thing on a page of a storybook. Have each child make a new sentence with the nouns he or she finds.

You Will Need

- Writer's Handbook, page 14
- chart paper and marker
- index cards with the following words written on them: *dog, cat, rat, ant, fox, hen, duck, pig, bug, bee, cow, bird, rug, hat, tree, can, pin, box, rock, fan, tub, sun, map, jar, pen, bag, mat, toy*
- paper and pencil for each child
- storybooks for noun identification
- tape

The(frog)sat on the(log).
The(cat)ran up the(tree).

✓ Assess Progress

Note whether children can recognize nouns. Provide additional practice if necessary.

Naming Words: People and Places (Proper Nouns)

Lesson Background

Proper nouns name specific people, places, or things. Unlike common nouns, which are written entirely in lowercase letters, the first letter of a proper noun must be capitalized.

Teaching the Lesson

- To introduce proper nouns, read aloud the relevant portions of pages 12 and 14 of the Writer's Handbook as children follow along.
- Explain that people's names and the names of specific places are naming words that follow a rule. Tell children that the names of people and places begin with a capital letter. Have volunteers state their names and the street they live on. Write the responses on chart paper, pointing out the capital letters.
- Write the word *boy* on chart paper. Ask children to name a boy in class. Write the child's name next to *boy*. Point out the initial capital letter. Repeat with *girl* and *teacher*.
- Write the word *school* on chart paper. Ask children to name their school. Write the school's name next to *school*. Point out the initial capital letter. Repeat with *city*.
- Explain proper nouns and capitalization. *Naming words name people, places, or things.* Words like girl *and* school *can tell us about many girls or schools, so they do not get capital letters. Words like* [name of girl in class] *and* [name of your school] *tell us the name of one girl or one school, so they begin with capital letters.*

Extending the Lesson

Write the following on chart paper: *girl, boy, teacher, city.* Read each noun aloud. Ask children to think of a name of another boy. Write the response next to *boy*, asking children what special thing you should do with the first letter. (capitalize it) Repeat with the remaining words.

On Your Own

Have each child make a list of five names of people they know and the name of one place. Remind them to capitalize the first letter of every name.

girl	(Ana)
boy	(Jake)
teacher	(Ms. Han)
city	(Memphis)

Assess Progress

Note whether children can recognize proper nouns and use capital letters appropriately. Provide additional practice if necessary.

Naming Words: Days, Months, Holidays

Lesson Background

Nouns name people, places, and things. Proper nouns have an initial capital letter because they are specific. The names of holidays, months, and days of the week are examples of proper nouns.

Teaching the Lesson

- To introduce calendar proper nouns, read aloud the relevant portions of pages 12–13 of the Writer's Handbook as children follow along.
- Write *day* and *Monday* on chart paper. Tell children that the two words are different kinds of naming words. Ask children which word stands for any day, and which names only one day of the week. When they answer, underline the capital *M* in *Monday*. Tell children that naming words that name something specific start with a capital letter.
- Draw a three-column chart. Label the columns *Day*, *Month*, and *Holiday*. Write *Monday* as the first example in the *Day* column. Repeat with *Month/May* and *Holiday/Thanksgiving*.
- Have children suggest other examples for each column. As you write their responses, ask children to identify which kind of first letter each naming word should have.
- Explain calendar proper nouns and their capitalization rules. *The words* day, month, *and* holiday *are naming words that do not get capital first letters, because they can name many things. Words like* Wednesday, August, *and* Thanksgiving *name only one thing, so they begin with capital letters.*

Extending the Lesson

Write the following word pairs on chart paper and have children identify which is correct: Week/week, Fourth of July/fourth of july, Sunday/sunday, April/april, Month/month.

On Your Own

Have each child write down the current day of the week, the current date, and his or her birthday. Remind children that days of the week and months need capital letters.

You Will Need

- Writer's Handbook, pages 12–13
- chart paper and marker
- paper and pencil for each child

Assess Progress

Note whether children recognize calendar proper nouns and capitalize them correctly. Provide additional practice if necessary.

Naming Words: Names and Titles

Lesson Background

Proper nouns have a capitalized initial letter because they name something specific. Specific names are capitalized, as are people's specific titles. Children should recognize names and titles and employ initial capital letters when writing them.

Teaching the Lesson

- To introduce proper nouns for names and titles, read aloud the relevant portions of pages 12–14 of the Writer's Handbook as children follow along.
- Write the following two sentences on chart paper and read them aloud: 1) *I go to the doctor.* 2) *I go to Doctor Tan.*
- Ask children which sentence tells the name, or title, of a specific person. Tell children that people's titles have capitalized first letters. Model writing two more titles of people children might know.
- Write *doctor, Doctor Tan, woman, Miss Duke, girl,* and *Nan* on chart paper and read them aloud. Ask children why *doctor* is not capitalized and *Doctor Tan* begins with a capital letter. Explain that people's names also have an initial capital letter because they name a specific person.
- Explain that names and titles are capitalized. *Names and titles that name one person need to start with a capital letter.*

Extending the Lesson

Name a common noun (*teacher, doctor, president*) and ask children to respond with a specific name or title that fits into that category. Record the names and titles children share in each category.

On Your Own

Have children create a "My Names and Titles" poster by drawing and labeling people they know. Write the sample list in the margin on chart paper as a guide. Remind children to capitalize the first letters of names and titles.

You Will Need

- Writer's Handbook, pages 12–14
- chart paper and marker
- pencil, large piece of paper, and drawing materials for each child

---

My Names and Titles

Tina

Doctor Lopez

Officer Martin

 **Assess Progress**

Note whether children properly capitalize names and titles. Provide additional practice if necessary.

Review All Naming Words

Lesson Background

Nouns name people, places, and things. Common nouns name general things, while proper nouns name specific people, places, days, months, holidays, and titles. Children should be familiar with both categories of nouns, and they should be able to capitalize the first letter of proper nouns.

Teaching the Lesson

- To review nouns, read aloud the relevant portions of pages 12–14 of the Writer's Handbook as children follow along.
- Ask children to clap when they hear a naming word. Read the sentence *The pig named Jill ran in the mud*. Write the three naming words on chart paper without capitalizing them: *pig, jill, mud*.
- Ask volunteers to identify which word should have a capital letter, then write the word *Jill*.
- Repeat with the next three sentences: 1) *Kip likes the Fourth of July.* 2) *Dallas is a big city.* 3) *Doctor Tan gave me a lollipop.*
- Review identification of nouns and the use of proper versus common nouns. *A naming word is the name of a person, animal, place, or thing. If a naming word names a person, place, day, month, holiday, or title, then the first letter of that naming word should be a capital letter.*

Extending the Lesson

Write the sentences in the margin on chart paper. Ask children to identify the naming words in each sentence. Underline the nouns. Then ask children to make up specific names for the general naming words (*e.g.,* Jamal went to Lincoln Park.) and write the resulting sentences on the chart paper.

On Your Own

Ask children to draw a picture of a person or animal in a place. They should label the person and place with common nouns (*e.g.,* cat, street) and proper nouns (*e.g.,* Fluffy, Wells Road). Ask early finishers to write a sentence about their picture.

You Will Need

- Writer's Handbook, pages 12–14
- chart paper and marker
- paper, pencil, and crayons for each child

The <u>boy</u> went to the <u>park</u>.

The <u>girl</u> likes a <u>holiday</u>.

The <u>family</u> saw a <u>movie</u>.

 **Assess Progress**

Note whether children can recognize different types of nouns and can capitalize when necessary. Provide additional practice if necessary.

Naming Words: One or More (Singular/Plural)

Lesson Background

Nouns name people, places, and things. Singular nouns name one item, and plural nouns name groups of items. Generally, singular nouns are made plural by the addition of an *-s* at the end of the word.

Teaching the Lesson

- To introduce singular and plural nouns, read aloud the relevant portion of page 14 of the Writer's Handbook as children follow along.
- Show children a toy car. Write the word *car* on chart paper. Show two cars. Add an *-s* to make *cars*. Ask a volunteer to tell why you added an *-s*.
- Hold up a book. Write *book* and say it. Hold up two books. Have a volunteer change the word to make it plural.
- Repeat with *hat* and *crayon*.
- Ask a volunteer to state what he or she noticed about changing a word from singular to plural in all the examples.
- Explain the difference between singular and plural nouns. *Some naming words name only one person, animal, place, or thing. Some naming words name more than one. You make most naming words name more than one by adding an* -s.

Extending the Lesson

Write the paragraph in the margin on chart paper. Read the paragraph aloud. Have children raise one finger when they hear a singular naming word and two fingers when they hear a plural naming word.

On Your Own

Ask children to choose an animal. Have them write it as a singular noun and illustrate it. Then ask them to do the same with its plural form.

You Will Need

- Writer's Handbook, page 14
- chart paper and marker
- two toy cars, two hats, two crayons, and two books
- paper, pencil, and drawing materials for each child

My <u>sister</u> takes me to the
zoo.
We see <u>pandas</u>.
Then we see <u>zebras</u>.
Next we see the <u>lion</u> and
her <u>cubs</u>.

 Assess Progress

Note whether children can identify and modify singular and plural nouns. Provide extra practice if necessary.

Action Words That Tell About Now (Present Tense)

Lesson Background

Verbs describe action or link a subject to other material in a sentence. Verbs can be conjugated to represent past, present, or future action. Verb tense indicates the time of the action.

Teaching the Lesson

- To introduce verbs in the present tense, read aloud the relevant portion of page 15 of the Writer's Handbook as children follow along.
- Ask a volunteer to sing a verse of a familiar song to the class. Write the following sentence on chart paper: [Child's name] *sings*. Explain to the class that *sing* is an action word that tells about now.
- Write *Action Words About Now* at the top of a sheet of chart paper.
- Call a child up to the front of the class. Ask the child to clap. Say [Child's name] *claps*. Explain to children that *claps* is another action word that tells about now. Write the verb on the chart.
- Repeat with other children, having one stomp his or her feet, tap his or her head, and wave hello. Call on children to describe what the child is doing using an action word about now. Write each verb on the chart.
- Explain verbs in the present tense. *Action words can tell us about something that is happening right now.*

Extending the Lesson

Ask children to write two action words for activities they enjoy doing (*e.g.*, swim, read). Have each child write a sentence explaining where he or she does each activity (*e.g.*, I swim in the pool.) in the present tense.

On Your Own

Have children make their own Action Words About Now charts. Write the paragraph in the margin on the chart paper. Then tell children to find the action words and add them to their own charts. Have children compare charts with a partner to check their answers.

We <u>play</u> tag.

We <u>run</u> fast.

We <u>go</u> far.

Then we <u>walk</u> home.

Assess Progress

Note whether children can identify present tense verbs. Provide additional practice if necessary.

Action Words That Tell About the Past (Past Tense)

Lesson Background

Verbs describe action or link a subject to other material in a sentence. Verbs can be conjugated to represent past, present, or future action. The past tense is used when writing about something that has already happened.

Teaching the Lesson

- To introduce verbs in the past tense, read aloud the relevant portion of page 15 of the Writer's Handbook as children follow along.
- Ask for a volunteer to say what game he or she played yesterday using a complete sentence. Explain that the child is using the action word *played* because the game already happened.
- Write *Action Words About the Past* at the top of a sheet of chart paper.
- Ask children to give examples of what they did yesterday. After each sentence, encourage children to identify the past tense verb in the sentence. Write that word on the chart.
- Underline the *–ed* at the end of each of the regular past tense verbs on the chart. Point out to children that past tense verbs usually end in *–ed*.
- Show children a page from a storybook that uses past tense. Pause after you read each sentence and encourage children to identify the past tense verbs. Add those verbs to the chart.
- Explain the past tense. *We use action words about the past to tell about something that has already happened.*

Extending the Lesson

Write the paragraph in the margin on chart paper and read it aloud. Ask children to identify the action words that tell about the past in the paragraph. Circle those words and add them to the chart.

On Your Own

Have children make their own Action Words About the Past chart. Then have them look through storybooks for past tense action words. Encourage children to add four words to their charts.

You Will Need

- Writer's Handbook, page 15
- chart paper and marker
- paper and pencil for each child
- storybooks for examples
- page from a storybook that uses the past tense

Rob and Lin (walked) to
the park.
They (played) tag.
Lin (tagged) Rob.

Assess Progress

Note whether children can identify past-tense verbs. Provide additional practice if necessary.

Review Action Words (Verbs)

Lesson Background

Action verbs describe action. Linking verbs link a subject to information about the subject. The present tense is used for action that is occurring now. The past tense is used for action that has already happened.

Teaching the Lesson

- To review present and past tenses, read aloud the relevant portion of page 15 of the Writer's Handbook as children follow along.
- Draw a T-chart on chart paper. Label the left column *Now* and the right column *The Past*. Walk slowly and in an exaggerated manner across the classroom. As you are walking, ask *What am I doing right now?* Write the word *walk* in the left column. Ask *What did I do before I wrote a word on the chart paper?* Write *walked* on the right side of the chart paper. Explain that action words can tell about now or about the past.
- Write the word *hug* in the *Now* column. Use it in a sentence. (*I hug my dad.*) Ask children to change the sentence to make it tell about the past. (*I hugged my dad.*) Ask children what is different about the two action words. Underline the *–ed* and explain that we can tell when action happened because now action words and action words about the past sound and look different.
- Explain to children the proper way to use past and present tenses. *We use action words about now when we are writing about something that is happening now. We use action words about the past when we are writing about something that has already happened. Action words about the past usually end in -ed.*

Extending the Lesson

Distribute index cards to children. Tell children that they have either an action word about now or an action word about the past. Explain that another child has the same action word that tells about a different time. Ask the children to find their action word partner and decide who has the word about now and who has the word about the past. Give them the hint that past action words usually end in *–ed*. Have the children tape their cards in the appropriate columns on the chart paper.

On Your Own

Ask children to pick an action word from the chart on the board. Have them write one sentence using the action word about now and one sentence using the action word about the past.

You Will Need

- Writer's Handbook, page 15
- chart paper and marker
- index cards with the following words written on them: *sip, sipped, rip, ripped, rake, raked, bake, baked, fan, fanned, sail, sailed, save, saved, yell, yelled, play, played, pull, pulled, tug, tugged, tap, tapped, talk, talked*
- tape
- paper and pencil for each child

Assess Progress

Note whether children can distinguish between present and past tense verbs. Provide additional practice if necessary.

Theme ⑩
Subject-Verb Agreement

Lesson Background

Subjects and verbs in any sentence must agree in number. Singular verbs are used with singular subjects. Plural verbs are used with plural subjects.

Teaching the Lesson

- To introduce subject-verb agreement, read aloud the relevant portion of page 5 of the Writer's Handbook as children follow along.
- Write the word *cat* on chart paper. Tell children that *cat* names one thing. Then ask a volunteer to add an *-s* to *cat* to make it name more than one. Say, *The naming word is cat. By adding -s, the naming word now means more than one cat.*
- Write the following sentences on chart paper: *The cat likes milk. The cats like milk.* Read the sentences aloud. Underline the subjects and circle the verbs in the sentences. Explain that *likes* goes with *cat* because they both talk about just one. *Like* goes with *cats* because they both talk about more than one.
- Explain to children how to use subjects and verbs. *Naming parts and action words must talk about the same number of things. When we add an -s to a naming word, it tells about more than one. When we add an -s to an action word, it tells about only one.*

Extending the Lesson

Have children write two sentences. The first (singular) sentence will tell about something an adult family member does at work. The second (plural) sentence will tell about something adults do at work. Have two volunteers read their sentences aloud.

On Your Own

Divide the class into pairs. Have each pair look through a storybook to find a sentence with a singular subject and one with a plural subject. Have pairs copy their sentences onto paper. Have them underline the subjects and label them either singular or plural.

You Will Need

- Writer's Handbook, page 5
- chart paper and marker
- storybooks for examples
- paper and pencil for each child

The cat <u>likes</u> milk.
The cats <u>like</u> milk.

Dad drives a truck.
All dads carry keys.

Assess Progress

Note whether children match singular and plural subjects and verbs. Provide additional practice if necessary.

Review Subject-Verb Agreement

Lesson Background

The subject and verb in any sentence must agree in number. Singular verbs are used with singular subjects. Plural verbs are used with plural subjects.

Teaching the Lesson

- To review subject-verb agreement, read aloud the relevant portion of page 5 of the Writer's Handbook as children follow along.
- Place index cards in two piles. Explain that one pile has naming word cards and the other has action word cards. Say that some cards tell about one and some cards tell about more than one.
- Have volunteers pick a card one at a time from each pile. Ask each child if the subject and verb on his or her cards agree or match (singular with singular, plural with plural), and why. If they do not agree, tell the child to choose two new cards.
- When the cards match, read aloud the cards. Then tape the cards to the board.
- Review singular and plural subjects and verbs and how to make sure that a subject and verb agree. *Adding an -s to most naming words makes them name more than one. Adding an -s to most action words makes them tell about one. When we write, naming words that tell about one have to be with action words that tell about one. Naming words about more than one must be with action words about more than one.*

Extending the Lesson

Divide the class into pairs. Assign each pair a plural word pair from the board. Ask the pairs to write a sentence using their assigned words.

On Your Own

Challenge children to change their assigned words to make both words only tell about one. Ask each pair to write a sentence with the new (singular) words.

You Will Need

- Writer's Handbook, page 5
- index cards with the following words written on them: *mother, mothers, father, fathers, boy, boys, girl, girls, teacher, teachers, baby, babies, kid, kids, take, takes, run, runs, see, sees, sit, sits, say, says, talk, talks, walk, walks*
- tape
- paper and pencil for each child

mother	runs
kids	run
teacher	talks
girls	talk
kid	sees

kids	sit
The kids sit in seats.	
kid	sits
The kid sits in a seat.	

✓ Assess Progress

Note children's ability to match subjects and verbs correctly. Provide additional practice if necessary.

Theme (11)

Subject Pronouns

Lesson Background

Pronouns replace nouns in order to avoid unnecessary repetition. A subject pronoun can act as the subject of a sentence in place of a noun that has already been named in the text.

Teaching the Lesson

- To introduce subject pronouns, read aloud the relevant portion of page 17 of the Writer's Handbook as children follow along.
- Write the following sentence on the board: <u>Ana</u> rides her bike. Read aloud the sentence. Tape the card that reads *She* on top of the word *Ana*. Read the sentence again, this time substituting *She* for *Ana*. Explain that *She* is a kind of word that can take the place of the naming word *Ana*.
- Tape the index cards on the board. Explain that these words can take the place of naming parts of sentences.
- Write the following sentences on the board:
  <u>Rob</u> sips water.
  <u>[Your name]'s class</u> read a book.
  <u>Jan and Yin</u> played tag.
  <u>The pail</u> is red.
- Ask children to find the pronoun that can replace each underlined subject. (*He, We, They, It*) Have children tape the card over the noun(s). Read each new sentence.
- Explain the proper way to use pronouns. *Some words can take the place of naming words and naming parts of sentences. These words include* I, you, he, she, it, we, *and* they.

Extending the Lesson

Write the paragraph in the margin on chart paper. Read it aloud. Then draw a two-column chart. Have children identify the subject pronouns in the paragraph. Circle them. Then have children identify the naming words they replaced. Underline them. Write the pronouns in one column and the nouns they replace in the other column.

On Your Own

Instruct children to make their own charts. Have children look through storybooks and ask them to find four examples of subject pronouns (*I, you, he, she, it, we, they*). Encourage children to use those words and the naming words they replace to fill out their charts.

You Will Need

- Writer's Handbook, page 17
- chart paper and marker
- index cards with the following words written on them: *I, You, He, She, It, We,* and *They*
- tape
- paper and pencil for each child
- storybooks for pronoun identification

<u>Dad and I</u> went to the park.	
(We) saw <u>Jon</u>.	
(He) said, "Hi."	
<u>Mom</u> came, too.	
(She) hugged Dad.	

We	Dad and I
He	Jon
She	Mom

Assess Progress

Note whether children can identify subject pronouns and the nouns they replace. Provide additional practice if necessary.

Object Pronouns

Lesson Background

Pronouns replace nouns in sentences. Object pronouns, such as *me*, *you*, *him*, *her*, *it*, *us*, and *them*, replace object nouns. These objects receive the action expressed by the sentence verb.

Teaching the Lesson

- To introduce object pronouns, read aloud the relevant portion of page 17 of the Writer's Handbook as children follow along.
- Write *Tom called Rosa* on chart paper. Read the sentence aloud. Tape the index card that says *her* on top of *Rosa*. Read the sentence again. Ask children what word *her* replaced. Explain that the action happens to a girl in the sentence, so you used *her* to replace *Rosa*.
- Tape the index cards with object pronouns on the board. Write a sentence referring to a volunteer, such as *Mom talked to* [child's name], on the chart paper. Have the named child come up and replace his or her name with the appropriate card and read the sentence aloud.
- Write the following sentences on the chart paper: *Emi wants <u>milk</u>. Ty reads to <u>[your name]'s class</u>. Andy talked to <u>Sari and Rick</u>.*
- For each sentence, ask a volunteer to replace the underlined part with a card. Have them tape the card over the naming word or words (*it, us, them*). Read the revised sentences, pointing out what each pronoun replaced.
- Explain when to use object pronouns. *Some words can take the place of naming words in sentences. The words* me, you, him, her, it, us, *and* them *take the place of naming words at the end of sentences.*

Extending the Lesson

Write the sentences in the margin on chart paper. Tape the object pronoun index cards next to them in random order. Ask children to use one of the words on the index cards to replace the naming word or words at the end of the sentence.

On Your Own

Ask children to draw a picture of themselves smiling at a family member or friend. Have them use an object pronoun to complete the sentence: *I smile at _____.*

You Will Need

- Writer's Handbook, page 17
- chart paper and marker
- index cards with the object pronouns *me, you, him, her, it, us,* and *them* written on them
- tape
- pencil, paper, and drawing materials for each child

I waved to <u>Lisa</u>. [her]

Ted reads to <u>Susan and Anna</u>. [them]

Ali plays with <u>a teddy bear</u>. [it]

[Your name] teaches <u>the children</u>. [us]

 **Assess Progress**

Note children's ability to replace object nouns with appropriate object pronouns. Provide additional practice if necessary.

Review Pronouns

Lesson Background

Pronouns replace nouns in sentences. Subject pronouns replace subjects. Object pronouns replace objects. Determining which pronouns are used for subjects and which for objects is necessary for grammatical accuracy.

Teaching the Lesson

- To review pronouns, read aloud the relevant portion of page 17 of the Writer's Handbook as children follow along.
- Tape index cards with *We, She, They,* and *He* on one side of the board and cards with *him, it, her,* and *them* on the other. Write *Deb helped Zack.* Ask children to determine who helped. Have a volunteer tape a subject pronoun (*She*) over *Deb.* Ask children who got help. Have another volunteer tape an object pronoun (*him*) over *Zack.*
- Repeat with these sentences: <u>First graders</u> read <u>books</u>. <u>Vin</u> eats <u>the soup</u>. <u>Nan and Tim</u> ate with <u>Lily</u>.
- Remind children how to use each kind of pronoun. *You can use words to replace naming words. When the naming word is at the beginning of the sentence, use* I, you, he, she, it, we, *or* they. *When the naming word is at the end of the sentence, use* me, you, him, her, it, us, *or* them.

Extending the Lesson

Have children stand in a circle and toss a beanbag to each other under your direction. After each toss, call on children to say who tossed the beanbag to whom, first using the children's names and then using pronouns.

On Your Own

Write the sentences in the margin on chart paper. Ask children to copy the sentences and rewrite them, replacing the nouns with pronouns.

Luke ate a carrot.

Liz plays with Ken.

[He ate it.]

[She plays with him.]

Assess Progress

Check that children can correctly replace nouns with subject and object pronouns. Provide extra practice if necessary.

Describing Words (Adjectives): Color and Size

Lesson Background

Adjectives modify nouns by adding description. They often give a physical description of an object. This lesson covers adjectives that describe the color and size of objects.

Teaching the Lesson

- To introduce adjectives, read aloud the relevant portion of page 18 of the Writer's Handbook as children follow along.
- Write on chart paper: *Jack has a _____ _____ cat.* Read the sentence aloud and ask children to close their eyes and visualize the cat.
- Add the words *small* and *black* in the blanks. Have children close their eyes and picture the cat again. Ask how the pictures in their minds changed when you added the adjectives. Repeat with *Sid threw a (tiny, green) ball* and *Mr. Han wore (long, red) socks*.
- Circle *small*, *tiny*, and *long* in the sentences above and read them aloud. Ask children what these words have in common. Write *Words That Tell Size* on the board, and add the three size words in a column underneath. Ask children to think of more words that fit. Add them to the list. Repeat for *Words That Tell Color*.
- Explain when to use adjectives. *Describing words tell more about naming words. You can use describing words to tell what color something is or what size it is.*

Extending the Lesson

Tell children to draw a circle and hold it up. Have them describe the color and size of the circle. Then ask children to draw a tiny green circle. Have children hold up both their drawings and describe their two circles.

On Your Own

Divide the class into pairs. Have each child tell his or her partner a color and a size. Each child must draw a house that fits his or her partner's adjectives. Then ask each child to write a sentence about his or her house that includes at least one color or size adjective.

You Will Need

- Writer's Handbook, page 18
- chart paper and marker
- pencil, two sheets of paper, and drawing materials (including a green crayon) for each child

Assess Progress

Note children's ability to use adjectives to describe color and size. Provide additional practice if necessary.

Describing Words (Adjectives): Feelings

Lesson Background

Adjectives modify nouns by adding description. In addition to physical descriptions, adjectives can describe feelings and emotions.

Teaching the Lesson

- To introduce adjectives that describe feelings, read aloud the relevant portion of page 18 of the Writer's Handbook as children follow along.
- Draw simple happy, sad, and mad faces on chart paper. Under each, write *This is a _____ face.* Model filling in the blank under the happy face. Ask volunteers to come up and complete the other two sentences.
- Write *Words That Tell About Feelings* on the chart paper and the three feeling words in a column underneath. Ask children to tell other feeling words that they know and add them to the list.
- Read the list together and talk about characters in books who have felt each of those feelings.
- Call up volunteers and whisper names of feelings for them to act out without words. Ask the class to guess the feeling, using adjectives.
- Explain how to describe feelings. *You can use describing words to tell how you or someone else feels.*

Extending the Lesson

Read aloud the paragraph in the margin. Have the children clap when they hear a feeling adjective. Write the paragraph on the chart paper and have volunteers underline the feeling words.

On Your Own

Ask children to draw themselves feeling *happy*, *sad*, or *mad*. Then have children copy and complete this sentence starter: *I feel _____ when I am at school.*

You Will Need

- Writer's Handbook, page 18
- chart paper and marker
- pencil, paper, and drawing materials for each child

I was <u>happy</u> at the circus. The tigers didn't make me feel <u>scared</u>. The popcorn was good. At the end, I felt <u>sad</u>.

 Assess Progress

Note children's ability to describe feelings with adjectives. Provide additional practice if necessary.

Describing Words (Adjectives): Senses

Lesson Background

Adjectives modify nouns or pronouns by adding description. Some adjectives describe what people see, hear, touch, taste, and smell.

Teaching the Lesson

- To introduce adjectives that describe senses, read aloud the relevant portion of page 18 of the Writer's Handbook as children follow along.
- Write *The Five Senses* on chart paper. Explain the five senses and write them in a row underneath the title. Ask children to point to the body part used for each sense.
- Ask children to think about a time when they watched someone make microwave popcorn. Have children use describing words to answer your questions. *How did the bag look? How did it sound when it was cooking? How did the popcorn smell? How did the popcorn feel in your hands? How did the popcorn taste?* Write the sense adjectives they share under the appropriate senses on the chart.
- Have children close their eyes and imagine seeing an object they like to look at. Ask volunteers to name their objects and tell you more about them with describing words. *I see a(n) _____ _____.* Write their adjectives on the chart. Then have them imagine hearing a sound they like. *I hear (an) _____ _____.* Repeat for all the senses.
- Tell children how to use adjectives to describe senses. *You can use describing words to tell about what you see, hear, feel, taste, and smell.*

Extending the Lesson

Ask children to work in pairs to add one sense adjective to the Five Senses chart. Children may repeat words used during the lesson or add new ones.

On Your Own

Ask children to think of a food they like to eat and have them write two sentences about it. Each sentence should use a sense adjective to describe the food.

The Five Senses				
Seeing	Hearing	Smelling	Feeling	Tasting
big	loud	yummy	rough	salty
red	quiet	stinky	soft	sweet

Assess Progress

Note children's ability to describe sensory input using adjectives. Provide additional practice if necessary.

Describing Words (Adjectives): How Many

Lesson Background

Adjectives modify nouns by adding description. Adjectives can describe quantity as well.

Teaching the Lesson

- To introduce adjectives that describe amounts, read aloud the relevant portion of page 18 of the Writer's Handbook as children follow along.
- Draw a group of three dots on one side of a sheet of chart paper. On the other side, draw a group of many dots. Under each group, write *There are _____ dots.* Read the sentences aloud.
- Point out to children that the two sentences are the same. Ask if the two drawings are the same.
- Write *a few* in the blank under the smaller group. Read the sentence. Ask children what can go in the blank of the other sentence. (*many*)
- Repeat with a drawing of two squares and a drawing of six squares. This time, use numbers as adjectives.
- Call up a small group and a larger group of children. Ask the class to use numbers and other adjectives to describe the two groups.
- Explain to children that adjectives can describe amounts. *You can use describing words to say how many of something there are.*

Extending the Lesson

Pass around a box of index cards with adjectives that describe amounts written on them. Ask children to tell about something they would like to have in the amount written on their index cards. For example, *I would like to have two dogs.*

On Your Own

Ask each child to write down the sentence that he or she just shared orally with the group. Children should underline the adjective. Early finishers may draw pictures to match their sentences.

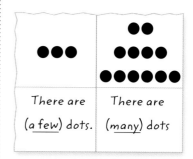

There are	There are
(a few) dots.	(many) dots

Note whether children can correctly use adjectives to describe amounts. Provide extra practice if necessary.

Review Adjectives

Lesson Background

Adjectives modify nouns by describing a noun's qualities. Children have learned about adjectives that describe color, size, feelings, the five senses, and amounts.

Teaching the Lesson

- To review adjectives, read aloud the relevant portion of page 18 of the Writer's Handbook as children follow along.
- Draw a five-column chart on chart paper. Label the columns *Color*, *Size*, *Feelings*, *Senses*, and *How Many*. Ask children to give an example of a describing word in each category.
- Tape a sentence strip to the board. Ask children for a describing word to fill in the blank. Write the word in the correct column on the chart. Ask children to provide two more describing words to fill in the blank. Add the adjectives to the chart. Repeat with the remaining sentence strips.
- Remind children when to use adjectives. *Describing words add details to your writing by telling about the naming words. You can use words to describe color, size, feelings, the five senses, and how many there are of something.*

Extending the Lesson

Create a "describing word snake" with the word *dog*. Write and circle *dog* on chart paper to make it the snake's head. As children suggest adjectives to describe *dog*, add them in a curvy chain to make the snake longer.

On Your Own

Ask children to write a sentence that uses at least one describing word from the chart paper. Tell children to exchange papers with a partner. Have partners read the sentences, circle the adjective(s) in the sentences, and underline the noun(s) they describe. Then have partners return the papers and check each other's work.

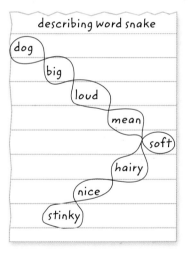

Assess Progress

Assess children's ability to use adjectives. Provide additional practice if necessary.

Review Simple Sentences

Lesson Background

A simple sentence expresses a complete idea. It includes a subject, a verb, and possibly an object. It begins with a capital letter and ends with a period, a question mark, or an exclamation point.

Teaching the Lesson

- To review simple sentences, read aloud the relevant portions of pages 4, 5, and 6 of the Writer's Handbook as children follow along.
- Hold up the word strip with *Sam* written on it. Read it aloud and ask children if *Sam* is a sentence. Have children explain their answers. Identify *Sam* as a naming part and tape it to the board. Hold up the *sings a song* word strip. Ask children if it is a sentence and have them explain their answers. Identify *sings a song* as a telling part and tape it to the board.
- Remind children that a sentence must have a naming part and a telling part to be complete. Ask children to tell if you should tape *sings a song* before *Sam* or after *Sam*. Tape the sentence strip in the appropriate spot and read aloud the full sentence.
- Ask children how they know that *Sam sings a song* is now a complete sentence. Have volunteers show the naming part, the telling part, the capital letter, and the period.
- Repeat with the strips that have *Sarah* and *claps her hands* written on them.
- Review the requirements for simple sentences. *A simple sentence uses a naming part and a telling part to tell one idea. It starts with a capital letter and ends with a period, a question mark, or an exclamation point.*

Extending the Lesson

Have each child write one sentence about himself or herself. Remind children that a sentence needs a capital letter and a punctuation mark.

On Your Own

Have children trade papers with a partner. Have children underline the naming parts of the sentences in blue and the telling parts in red. Have children circle the initial capital letter in green and the punctuation mark in orange.

You Will Need

- Writer's Handbook, pages 4, 5, and 6
- chart paper and marker
- word strips with the following written on them:
  Sam
  Sarah
  sings a song.
  claps her hands.
- tape
- a piece of paper, pencil, and four crayons (blue, red, green, and orange) for each child

Assess Progress

Note children's ability to create simple sentences. Provide additional practice if necessary.

Join Simple Sentences with *and*

Lesson Background

A compound sentence uses a conjunction to join two or more simple sentences that could otherwise stand on their own. This lesson focuses on joining two simple sentences with a comma and the conjunction *and*.

Teaching the Lesson

- To introduce compound sentences, read aloud the relevant portion of page 6 of the Writer's Handbook as children follow along.
- Tape the two sentence strips on chart paper so that they are side-by-side with a small space between them. Read them together.
- Ask volunteers how they can tell that the two sentences are each complete sentences. Guide them to include the fact that they have naming parts, telling parts, initial capital letters, and periods.
- Ask children to imagine that Sam is singing while Sarah is clapping. Tell children that by connecting these sentences with the joining word *and* and a comma we can show that the events are happening at the same time. Hold the index card with the word *and* between the two sentences and read aloud the resulting sentence.
- Model rewriting the new compound sentence by omitting the first period and inserting a comma and the word *and*.
- Explain how to use *and* to form a compound sentence. *You can put two sentences together using a comma and a joining word like* and *to create one longer sentence.*

Extending the Lesson

Ask children to write a short sentence about an animal doing something at the zoo. Have two children at a time read their sentences. As the first child finishes his or her sentence, have both partners say *and* before the second sentence is read.

On Your Own

Divide the class into pairs. Ask partners to rewrite their two zoo sentences to form one compound sentence. Remind children to use capital letters and punctuation correctly in their new sentences. Have two volunteers read their new compound sentence to the class.

You Will Need

- Writer's Handbook, page 6
- chart paper and marker
- sentence strips with the following written on them:
  Sam sings a song.
  Sarah claps her hands.
- index card with a comma and the word *and* written on it
- tape
- pencil and paper for each child

> The lion roars.
>
> A monkey climbs a tree.
>
> The lion roars, and
>
> a monkey climbs a tree.

Assess Progress

Note children's ability to join simple sentences with *and*. Provide additional practice if necessary.

Review Simple and Compound Sentences

Lesson Background

A simple sentence uses a subject and a predicate to express one complete idea. The predicate contains a verb and may contain an object. Combining two simple sentences with a comma and a conjunction creates a compound sentence. Children have been taught to form compound sentences using a comma and the word *and*.

Teaching the Lesson

- To review simple and compound sentences, read aloud the relevant portion of page 6 of the Writer's Handbook as children follow along.
- Tape animal pictures on the board. Post the *I hop in the yard* sentence strip on the board. Ask the children if this is a sentence. Have them explain their answers. Guide them to include the fact that it has a naming part, a telling part, a capital letter, and a period. Read the sentence again, and ask children to tell which animal it describes. (could describe any of them)
- Tape the second sentence strip (*I eat a carrot*) over the first. Repeat the exercise.
- Now post both sentence strips side-by-side. Say, *I wonder if putting these simple sentences together will make it easier to tell who the animal is.* Rewrite the sentences into one compound sentence joined with a comma and the word *and*.
- Read the new sentence with children. Ask children to tell which animal is described in the new compound sentence.
- Explain simple sentences and compound sentences. *A simple sentence uses a naming part and a telling part to make a complete thought. You can join two simple sentences together with the word* and *to make a longer sentence.*

Extending the Lesson

Divide the class into pairs. Have partners choose an animal from the board and write two sentences about it. Pairs should then rewrite their sentences into one compound sentence using the word *and*.

On Your Own

Write on chart paper and read aloud the sentences in the margin. Ask children to write two sentences about themselves and then rewrite them into a compound sentence using *and*.

You Will Need

- Writer's Handbook, page 6
- chart paper and marker
- animal pictures, including a frog, a rabbit, and a cat
- tape
- sentence strips with the following written on them:
  I hop in the yard.
  I eat a carrot.
- pencil and paper for each child

I am smart.

I like to read.

I am smart and I like to read.

Assess Progress

Note whether children can create simple and compound sentences. Provide additional practice if necessary.

Sequence Organizer

First

Next

Then

Finally

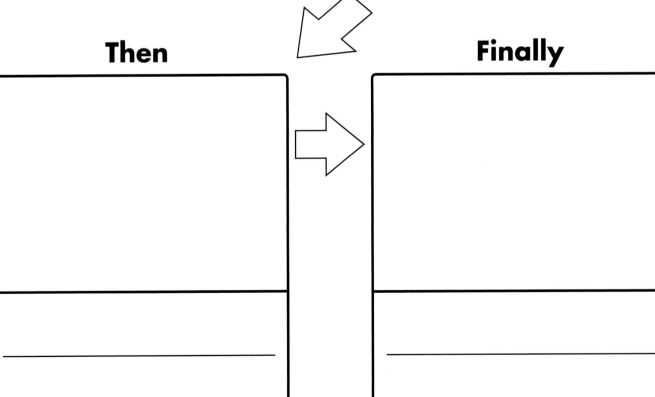

Name _____ Date _____

Report Organizer

Title

_____

Main Idea

_____

Facts

1. _____

_____

_____

2. _____

_____

_____

Name _____ Date _____

Story Organizer

Beginning

_____

_____

Middle

_____

_____

End

_____

_____

Name _____ Date _____

Sequence Organizer

First

Next

_____

_____

Then

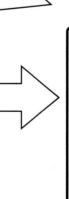

Finally

_____

_____

Sequence Organizer

Name _____ Date _____

Story Organizer

_____

Beginning

_____

_____

Middle

_____

_____

End

_____

_____

Name _____ Date _____

Main Idea and Details Organizer

Main Idea

_____

_____

```
        ↓               ↓
```

Detail

_____

_____

_____

Detail

_____

_____

_____

Main Idea and Details Organizer

Name _____ Date _____

Poem Organizer

Descriptive Words

_____

_____

_____

_____

_____

Name _____ Date _____

Main Idea and Details Organizer

Topic _____

Main Idea _____

Details

1. _____

_____

_____

2. _____

_____

_____

3. _____

_____

Main Idea and Details Organizer

Problem and Solution Organizer

Problem

Solution

Name _____ Date _____

Personal Narrative Organizer

First	What Happened:
	_____
	My Feelings:
	_____

Next	What Happened:
	_____
	My Feelings:
	_____

Then	What Happened:
	_____
	My Feelings:
	_____

Personal Narrative Organizer

Name _____ Date _____

Letter Organizer

Date

Greeting

Body

Closing

Signature

Procedural Text Organizer

How to

_____

You Need

_____

_____

Step 1

_____

_____

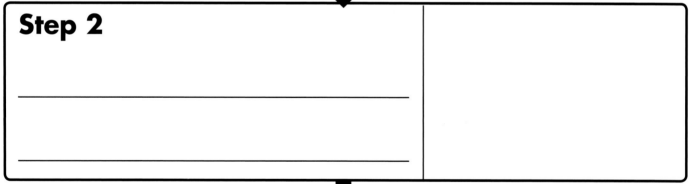

Step 2

_____

_____

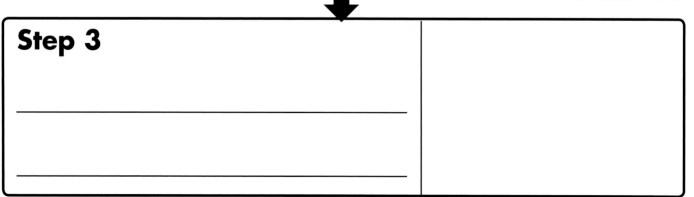

Step 3

_____

_____

Problem and Solution Organizer

Problem

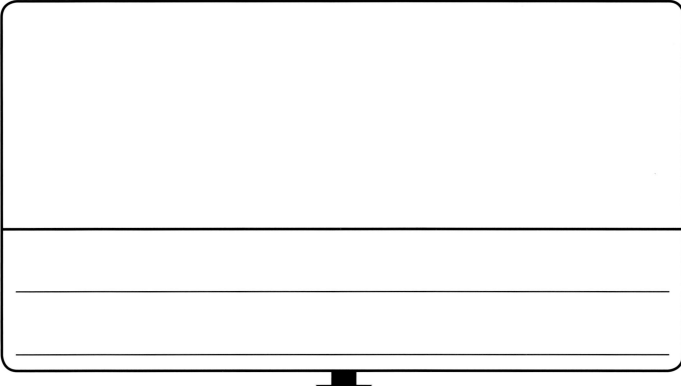

Solution

Name _____ Date _____

Report Organizer

Title

_____

Main Idea

_____

Facts

1. _____

   _____

   _____

2. _____

   _____

   _____

Story Organizer

[ ]

Beginning

_____

_____

Middle

_____

_____

End

_____

_____

Name _____ Date _____

Main Idea and Details Organizer

Topic _____

Main Idea _____

Supporting Details

1. _____

   _____

   _____

2. _____

   _____

   _____

3. _____

   _____

Make Your Ideas Clear

Lesson Background

A strong paragraph contains a main idea and supporting details. Introduce paragraphs as groups of sentences that have a main idea that connects them.

Teaching the Lesson

- Copy and distribute the Build Strong Paragraphs Master on page 50 of this guide. You may wish to make a transparency of this page for use during whole-class instruction.
- Read the selection "My Cat" aloud as children follow along.
- After reading, discuss the selection with children. Ask *What is this story about?* (someone's cat) *Are all of the sentences about the same thing?* (yes) *What are all of the sentences about?* (a cat)
- Tell children that paragraphs have sentences that are all about the same thing. The first sentence tells the reader what the rest of the paragraph will be about. This is called the main idea. As a class, brainstorm a main idea sentence about school and write the children's response on chart paper. Also discuss possibilities for appropriate sentences to follow the main idea sentence.
- Have partners write three sentences about a place they like to go. Remind them that the sentences must be about the same place.

Extending the Lesson

During small-group writing instruction, have children select a recent piece of writing from their writing folders and identify the main idea. Support children as they revise their writing to put the main idea first. Then compare both versions as a group.

On Your Own

Have children look through other books or stories in the classroom to find a paragraph they like. Encourage children to copy the paragraph into their Writer's Notebook as a paragraph example.

Assess Progress

Note whether children are able to craft paragraphs that include a main idea and details. Provide additional practice if necessary.

My Cat

I have a cat.

His fur is black and white.

My cat is funny!

Put Sentences Together

With a partner, write three sentences about a place you like to go. Make sure the sentences are about the same place.

_____

_____

_____

_____

Build Strong Paragraphs Master

Create an Atmosphere

Lesson Background

Writers establish a setting by creating an atmosphere that encourages and allows readers to "see" where and when a story takes place. Introduce setting by having children identify the settings in texts and in their own stories.

Teaching the Lesson

- Copy and distribute the Establish Setting Master on page 52 of this guide. You may wish to make a transparency of this page for use during whole-class instruction.
- Read the selection "Our Class Trip" aloud as children follow along.
- After reading, discuss the selection with children. Ask *What is the story about?* (a trip) *Does the story tell us where the class went on the trip?* (no) *How could we improve the story so that it tells us where the class went?* (name the place)
- Tell children that writers should make sure that readers know where and when a story takes place. Write the following on chart paper: *I went to the park on Saturday.* Say *This tells us where the writer went.* Circle *the park.* Say *It also tells us when the writer went there.* Underline *Saturday.*
- As a class, brainstorm ways to include the setting in the first sentence of "Our Class Trip."
- Have children edit "Our Class Trip" by rewriting the first sentence to include the setting. Have them draw an illustration that shows where the story took place.

Extending the Lesson

During small-group writing instruction, have children select a recent piece of writing from their writing folders that needs to show where and when the story took place. Support children as they revise their writing. Then compare the original and revised versions as a group.

On Your Own

Have partners draw a picture that shows where something took place (*e.g.,* a sporting event, carnival, swimming party). Then have partners exchange pictures and tell each other where and when the event in the picture took place.

Assess Progress

Note whether children are able to establish setting in their writing. Provide additional practice if necessary.

Our Class Trip

We went on a trip.

We saw lions and tigers.

We saw bears and hippos.

I liked the monkeys the best.

Write the Setting

Rewrite the first sentence of "Our Class Trip" so that it tells where and when the story took place.

_____

_____

_____

On a separate sheet of paper, draw a picture that shows where "Our Class Trip" took place.

Establish Setting Master

Spice Up Your Story with Conversation

Lesson Background

Writers can use dialogue to develop their characters. Dialogue makes a story richer and enhances the plot. Writers use quotation marks and the word *said* to add dialogue to a story. For beginning writers, recognizing quotation marks is an important step toward using this convention in their writing.

Teaching the Lesson

- Copy and distribute the Incorporate Dialogue Master on page 54 of this guide. You may wish to make a transparency of this page for use during whole-class instruction.
- Read the selection "The New Hat" aloud as children follow along.
- After reading, discuss the selection with children. Ask *What is the story about?* (getting a hat) *Who are the characters?* (Min and Mom) *What do they say to each other?* (Pick the hat you like. I like the red hat.) Draw the two characters on chart paper with talk bubbles next to each of them. Write what each character says in the bubbles.
- Tell children that dialogue is what writing is called when characters in a story are talking. Draw quotation marks around the dialogue in the talk bubbles and explain that writers put quotation marks around words to show when people begin and end what they are saying. Add *she said* to the end of each sentence. Explain that the word *said* tells who is speaking.
- Have children circle the quotation marks and underline *said* in "Mom's New Hat" together.

Extending the Lesson

During small-group writing instruction, have children select a recent piece of writing from their writing folders that they think would be improved by having characters speak. Support children as they revise their writing. Then compare both versions as a group.

On Your Own

Have partners take turns telling each other one sentence about an activity they enjoy doing on the weekend. Tell children that each partner should draw the other partner with a talk bubble and write down the sentence the partner stated. Have them rewrite the sentence on lined paper, adding quotation marks and identifying the speaker with *said*.

Assess Progress

Note whether children are able to incorporate dialogue into their stories. Provide additional practice if necessary.

The New Hat

Mom will buy Min a new hat.

"Pick the hat you like," Mom said.

"I like the red hat," said Min.

Use Dialogue

Circle the quotation marks and underline the word *said*.

Mom's New Hat

Mom wants a new hat, too.

"Pick a color," Min said.

"I like the black hat," Mom said.

Incorporate Dialogue Master

Stress What's Important

Lesson Background

Writers often repeat sounds (assonance), first letters (alliteration), and words to create rhythm, rhyme, and emphasis in poetry and children's stories. Beginning writers can learn to recognize these techniques and use repetition in their own writing.

Teaching the Lesson

- Copy and distribute the Use Repetition for Emphasis Master on page 56 of this guide. You may wish to make a transparency of this page for use during whole-class instruction.
- Read the selection "Poor Pat!" aloud as children follow along.
- After reading, discuss the selection with children. Ask *Who is Pat?* (a cat) *What happened to the hat?* (she lost it) *How did Pat feel?* (sad)
- Tell children that writers often repeat sounds and words in poems and stories to stress what is important and to make the poem or story more fun to read. Ask children what sound gets repeated a lot in the story. Have them underline all the *-at* sounds. Ask children why *sad* is repeated three times. (to let the reader know just how sad Pat is)
- Have children work with a partner to write two sentences containing words with the *-an* sound.

Extending the Lesson

During small-group writing instruction, have children select a recent piece of writing from their writing folders and add repeated sounds or words. Support children as they revise their writing. Then compare the original and revised versions as a group.

On Your Own

Have children look through storybooks to find repeated words or sounds that make a story or poem fun to read. Encourage children to record some of these in their Writer's Notebook as examples of repetition.

Assess Progress

Note whether children are able to repeat elements in their writing to create rhyme and emphasis. Provide additional practice if necessary.

Poor Pat!

Pat the cat had a hat.

Poor Pat lost that hat.

She was sad, sad, sad!

Use Words That Rhyme

Work with a partner to write two sentences about a boy named Dan. Use words from the box to help you repeat the *-an* sound.

can	fan	pan
ran	tan	van

_____

_____

_____

_____

Engage Your Reader with a Lively Beginning

Lesson Background

Strong beginnings are one of the most important aspects of good writing. They guide readers into the piece of writing and spark their interest. One of the ways a writer can draw readers into a story is through action. This lesson focuses on the strategy of starting strong by using action.

Teaching the Lesson

- Copy and distribute the Start Strong Master on page 58 of this guide. You may wish to make a transparency of this page for use during whole-class instruction.
- Find a familiar storybook that begins with action. Draw a big fish on chart paper and write the opening sentence next to the fish. Draw a fishing pole and hook next to the fish.
- Tell children *Good openings are like using hooks to catch fish. When you "hook" your readers with your first sentence, you catch them as you would fish. The hook grabs readers and makes them want to read more.* Have children hook their fingers and show their neighbor how a hook catches a fish.
- Tell children one way to make openings exciting is by showing an action that is happening.
- Read "The Race" aloud as children follow along. Guide children to brainstorm possible opening action sentences for "The Race." Write their ideas on chart paper. You may wish to suggest the following: *Ready? Set! Go!* or *I started to run and pump my arms.*
- Have children write a new beginning sentence for "The Race" that includes action.

Extending the Lesson

During small-group writing instruction, have children select a recent piece of writing from their writing folders that they think needs action at the beginning. Support children as they rewrite their beginning sentences. Then compare the original and revised versions as a group.

On Your Own

Have children look through other books to find openers that really "hook" their attention. Encourage children to record some of these in their Writer's Notebook as examples of effective openers. Children may also wish to draw a fish and hook in their Writer's Notebook to remind them about good opening sentences.

Assess Progress

Note whether children are able to recognize and craft lively beginnings by opening with action. Provide additional practice if necessary.

The Race

There was a race.

My friends and I ran to the finish line.

We did our best.

But guess who won? I did!

Show Action

Write a new beginning sentence for "The Race" that will "hook" the reader with action.

_____

_____

_____

Aim at the Right Target

Lesson Background

Writers must think about their reason, or purpose, for writing as well as their intended audience. The first step to learning these fundamental writing strategies is recognizing them in others' work.

Teaching the Lesson

- Copy and distribute the Adapt to Purpose and Audience Master on page 60 of this guide. You may wish to make a transparency of this page for use during whole-class instruction.
- Read the selections "Letter to Mom" and "My Favorite Part of the Day" aloud as children follow along.
- After reading, discuss the selections with children. Ask *Were these two pieces written for the same reason?* (no) Tell children that these two selections show that writers write different pieces for different reasons. Ask *Why do you think someone would write a letter to his or her mom?* (The author wants to tell his or her mom something.) *Why would someone write about his or her favorite part of the school day?* (It was written for school.)
- Ask *Who is the letter supposed to be for?* (Mom) *Who do you think will read "My Favorite Part of the Day"?* (teacher) Tell children that writers think about who will be reading their work. Writers change their writing depending on who is reading the selection. Say *The letter to Mom says* I love you, *but the paragraph for school doesn't.*
- Have children compose two sentences about an activity they like to do. Remind them to think about why they are writing the sentences (for school) and who will read them (the teacher).

Extending the Lesson

During small-group writing instruction, have children select a recent piece of writing from their writing folders. Direct children to reread their work and decide why it was written and who will read it.

On Your Own

Have partners each write a letter to a relative or friend. Then have them exchange papers and share with each other who the letter was written to and why they wrote it.

Assess Progress

Note whether children are able to identify the purpose and intended audience of different writing pieces. Provide additional practice if necessary.

Letter to Mom

Dear Mom,

I love you very much.

You are the best mom in the world.

Love,
Eva

My Favorite Part of the Day

Name: Maya Novo   Date: May 4, 2008

My favorite part of the day is recess.

You get to play with your friends.

I will always love recess.

Explain What You Like

On a separate sheet of paper, write two sentences about something you like to do. Think about who will read your writing and why you are writing it.

Finish on a Strong Note

Lesson Background

Strong endings can help a writer keep the reader's attention, drive home a point, or make a piece of writing memorable. For beginning writers, an effective ending completes the sequence of events. Conflicts are resolved, and the plot is finished.

Teaching the Lesson

- Copy and distribute the End Effectively Master on page 62 of this guide. You may wish to make a transparency of this page for use during whole-class instruction.
- Read the selection "The Gift" aloud as children follow along.
- After reading, discuss the selection with children. Ask *What is the story about?* (a gift) *Does the writer finish the story?* (no) *How could the ending be better?* (it could say what the gift is) *How could it answer any questions we may have as readers?* (name the gift)
- Tell children that writers must finish their stories. For example, when there is a problem, the writer should tell how the problem is resolved. Brainstorm with children effective ending sentences that help finish the writing piece "The Gift."
- Have children write an ending sentence for "The Gift." Children may record a class suggestion or write a new ending sentence of their own.

Extending the Lesson

During small-group writing instruction, have children select a recent piece of writing from their writing folders that they think needs a new ending. Support children as they revise their writing. Have them write their new ending on a sticky note to attach to their writing.

On Your Own

Have children look through storybooks to find endings that complete the story. Encourage children to record some of these in their Writer's Notebook as examples of effective endings.

 **Assess Progress**

Note whether children are able to craft effective endings. Provide additional practice if necessary.

The Gift

Grandma sent me a gift.

It came in the mail.

It was a big box.

I opened it.

Finish the Story!

Write an ending sentence for "The Gift."

_____

_____

_____

End Effectively Master

Breathe Life into the People in Your Stories

Lesson Background

Writers build characters by using dialogue and by describing characters'
appearances, actions, emotions, motivations, and reactions to one another.
This lesson focuses on the strategy of building characters by describing
their actions.

Teaching the Lesson

- Copy and distribute the Build Characters Master on page 64 of this guide.
  You may wish to make a transparency of this page for use during
  whole-class instruction.
- Read the selection "Miles" aloud as children follow along.
- After reading, ask the children how they would show that Miles is liked by
  everyone if they were to draw a picture of him. Ask *How could you show
  that he helps everyone? How could you show that he shares his toys?* Draw or
  have a volunteer draw class suggestions on chart paper.
- Tell children *Writers help us understand the people in their stories by showing
  us what actions the people do. By reading what someone does, we can get to
  know the person better. When we read about Miles, we can tell he is nice by
  the nice things he does. He helps his friends and shares his toys.*
- Have a volunteer describe the actions of a person he or she thinks is a
  good friend. Write the descriptions on a new piece of chart paper. You
  may wish to suggest behavior examples such as taking turns, asking you
  to be on her team, or eating lunch with you.
- Have children write two sentences about a good friend that describe the
  friend's actions.

Extending the Lesson

During small-group writing instruction, have children select a recent piece
of writing from their writing folders and add a sentence that shows the
way a character acts. Support children as they revise their writing. Then
compare the original and revised versions as a group.

On Your Own

Have children draw a picture of a favorite character from a book. Then have
them write two sentences describing the character with examples of what
the character does.

Assess Progress

Note whether children are able to
develop characters through action.
Provide additional practice if
necessary.

Miles

Miles is very nice.

He always helps his friends.

He shares his toys.

Everyone likes him.

Say What Friends Do

Write two sentences about a good friend. Make sure to tell the things a good friend does.

_____

_____

_____

_____

Build Characters Master

Editing Checklist

☐ My name is on my writing piece.

☐ My writing piece has a title.

☐ I read over my piece twice.

☐ I read my piece to a friend.

☐ There are spaces between the words.

☐ The first letter of each sentence is a capital letter.

☐ Each sentence has a . ? or !

☐ I have tried to spell the words by sounding them out.

☐ This is my best work.

Writer's Reflection Checklist

☐ What I wrote about: _____

_____

☐ This is one way I made my piece better: _____

_____

☐ My favorite part of my writing is: _____

_____

☐ I shared my writing with _____

_____

☐ One thing I learned about writing was: _____

_____

Writing Traits Checklist

Ideas

☐ My writing has a point or tells a story.

☐ I used details or pictures to support my writing.

Organization

☐ My words and sentences are in an order that makes sense.

☐ I put a title on my work.

Voice

☐ My writing sounds like me.

☐ I let my feelings show in my writing.

Word Choice

☐ I used words that describe or paint a picture.

☐ I used action words.

☐ I used good naming words.

Sentence Fluency

☐ I used complete sentences.

☐ I used connecting words to make my writing flow.

Conventions

☐ I checked my spelling.

☐ I began each sentence with a capital letter.

☐ I used a . ? or ! at the end of each sentence.

Presentation

☐ My writing is neat and clear.

☐ I added pictures or drawings to my work.

Writer's Craft Checklist

☐ My writing piece has a beginning.

☐ My piece makes sense.

☐ My writing piece is in order.

☐ I know who will read my piece and why I wrote it.

☐ My piece has a setting (time and place).

☐ I have interesting characters in my piece.

☐ I used interesting words.

☐ My sentences are all about the same thing.

☐ My writing piece has an ending.

☐ My pictures match my writing piece.